The Way to Stillness

POWERFUL TOOLS FOR THOSE IN HELPING PROFESSIONS

The Way to
Stillness

POWERFUL TOOLS FOR THOSE
IN HELPING PROFESSIONS

GAYLE ALEXANDER AND
ANNE ALEXANDER VINCENT

The Way To Stillness
Powerful Tools For Those In Helping Professions

Copyright Anne Alexander Vincent

ISBN: 978-0-9840876-0-0

Authors Anne Alexander Vincent & Gayle Alexander
Design Anne LoCascio
Photos used with permission of Jupiter Unlimited
Story of the Bells by Anthony De Mello used by permission.
Anne and Gayle wish to thank Amy Collins MacGregor of The Cadence
Group for her encouragement, diligence, and expertise on this project.

Published by Cottage In The Woods
Nashville, TN, USA

Printed in Canada

Gayle wishes to dedicate the Way to Stillness
to her late husband, Dr. David K. Alexander,
and to her three daughters Anne, Jane, and Beth.

A Special Thanks to Grace Hall.

In the depth of winter, I finally learned

that within me there lay

an invincible summer.

—Albert Camus

ABOUT GAYLE ALEXANDER

Gayle Alexander may well have coined the term psycho-educational counseling—a blend of depth psychology (as influenced by Jung), educational skill development, and her own mental, spiritual, and emotional approaches to enrich people's personal and professional lives.

Considered to be a pioneer in this area, she and her husband, David, built a retreat center in the hills of Tennessee in 1956. Over the course of fifty years, this was a home for her counseling practice serving individuals and families from throughout the U.S. and far-reaching parts of the world.

Inspired by their faith, courage, and by something Gayle calls the Love Motif, Gayle and David were strengthened by their opportunities to learn first-hand from some of the great souls of our time such as Mother Teresa and Viktor Frankl.

As Gayle retired from full-time active practice as a counselor, her work has been carried on by her daughters.

STORY OF THE BELLS

There once was an island temple filled with beautiful bells. When great winds rushed through the temple the bells would ring out for miles around bringing joy into the hearts of those who listened.

It is said that over time, though the temple island was swallowed by the sea, the bells continued to ring out, even as they were now deep beneath the ocean's surface. Hearing of the legend, a young man set out on a great journey to hear the bells. He waited by the nearest shore and listened. Yet, he heard nothing but the sea in spite of his efforts to block its sound.

For weeks and weeks he listened for those bells. Finally, he was ready to give up. But on his last day, as he breathed in the fresh ocean air, he listened to the sea for the first time. As this sound flowed through him he fell into a deeper place within himself. And it was here that he suddenly heard the faint ringing of one bell, then another, and then a choir of bells infusing him with joy and self-awareness.

by Anthony De Mello

THE *Love* MOTIF

The primary goal for our counseling practice is that each individual find and embrace all that which is in them as truly good. It is my hope that their hearts and their minds work in parallel—in sync. My wish for them is that they achieve the purpose of their life.

Each day, this goal has expressed my desire to help enable each person to get in touch with what is within them, to give them joy and fulfillment in life. My highest goal is to help others find that peace.

What is woven throughout this goal is the concept of the Love Motif. The Love Motif is offering not only our best and healthiest self to another, but also allowing them the freedom to be who they are without limit or condition. The power of the Love Motif will unlock the human mind and spirit and enable people to transcend their circumstances.

THE STORY OF MIKE

Mike was a legally blind young boy from an economically disadvantaged home in the rural south. Somewhere in first grade the schools had given up on him. Students and teachers had pushed him aside saying, "Never mind Mike, he can't read." And Mike cooperated—if he "couldn't read," he wouldn't read.

Dr. Kirk, a psychiatrist at Vanderbilt had worked and worked with this boy and had been unable to determine why he was not reading. She heard that I had a special gift for teaching kids to read, and asked me to assist.

Mike's family drove him from Kentucky to Nashville to meet with me. Since it was all they could do to put together the gas money for the drive to Nashville, I knew I had to make every moment count. We started talking and Mike expressed an interest in machines. I checked with his parents and took him down to the boiler room at

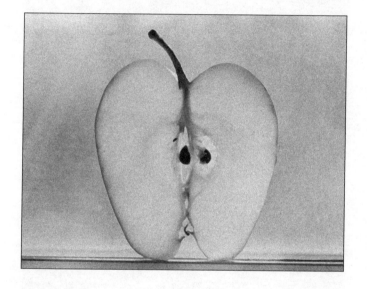

Peabody College on the campus of Vanderbilt University, where we went in and asked to meet the engineer.

The engineer was a patient man with a wonderful heart, and Mike asked him all sorts of wonderful questions about the boiler and the heat it was radiating. The engineer allowed Mike to touch and explore the machinery—and I realized that Mike intuitively knew more about science than he could learn from any book. He already knew more than many students at the graduate level, and here he was coming to me because his school thought him slow!

His parents found the gas money to bring him back again the next week and at the next session, I gave him an article on heat. I told him "Don't read it. Just look at the words that you can make out." He started picking out just choice words so that he could get the idea, and of course, he could tell I knew nothing about the subject. Here, with my complete ignorance of this subject, was a boy who knew so much.

I thought to myself "He is my teacher! Here I am with this treasure, this miracle in my hands!"

After some time his teacher from Russellville, Kentucky called me, amazed at his improvement, saying, "This boy's never read before, and suddenly, he's scanning the material in class and raising his hand to respond to my questions. The other kids just look at him now in disbelief. I have to look at the book just to stay ahead of him!"

It was disturbing to me because it happened so fast. These wonderful things were happening for Mike and I knew they were real; yet, it seemed like magic, and I had difficulty accounting for everything that was happening. I wasn't completely sure what to think. I experienced great self-doubt because the results of my work with Mike far exceeded what I had believed possible.

One of the things that made me more comfortable with Mike's turnaround was this: I had invited Dr. Lillian Bloeschl to come to Nashville. She was in charge of counseling at the University of Graz in Austria. I had met her there, and invited her to spend a month here in Nashville. Having sat in on one of my sessions with Mike she said, "You know, Gayle, you don't have to know clinically

what's happening here—it's enough to know that Mike is now reading at grade level and beyond."

But I wanted to fully understand how I was able to achieve these results, and I couldn't. "Lillian," I said, "If I could explain this scientifically, it would be one thing, but I feel kind of like the medicine man at the circus or a magician at the carnival that magically unlocks the box through some kind of trick. What's happening here that this boy can read?"

Mike's success was not coming from me.

Many individuals struggle to function in a normal, socially prescribed manner, and as a result are marginalized by themselves or others, and end up falling far short of their true potential as human beings. It is our premise that, to a great extent, these people are missing a certain intangible spiritual quality. So when they act in particularly inappropriate or "abnormal" ways, it is often because of this spiritual deficit. If we could fill that deficit with enough love that they could be nourished by it, then a spiritual bridge would be built between us. That is the essence of the Love Motif.

I quickly came to see that Mike's success was a direct result of our application of the Love Motif. I came to realize that it is *being with* another person and being *thoroughly present* that can be transforming. In essence, the Love Motif is meeting people where they are. It is about communicating and participating with them in their own language and on their own non-threatening and intrinsically self-validating terms.

Our work is about creating a conduit through which the Love Motif can become operational. This conduit leads to the reduction of fear, development of trust, willingness to make life changes, and a commitment to follow through on one's dreams and be personally accountable to another person. This can then serve as a model for further accountability in the lives of those counseled. Being an effective conduit means allowing ourselves to become an instrument for a power greater than ourselves, in order to achieve greater results in any given relationship.

One spring morning, I received an invitation to attend Mike's high school graduation ceremony in the heart of the hills of Kentucky. Mike graduated from high school! Years before, I had worked with the principal, asking that Mike not be passed on to another grade unless it was on merit. They didn't just pass him on. He seemed to take off in the sciences, and this success helped him get through the other courses. It was his work and his marks that got him through.

OTHER ELEMENTS
OF THE LOVE MOTIF

In all the psychology courses that I took, in my pursuit of understanding, I realized that there is something more. I realized that not only are we, as counseling psychologists and helping professionals, being entrusted with the private details of a person's factual past, we are also being entrusted with various levels of their personal experience. In order to be the best possible counselor for a given client, we need to be totally comfortable when talking with them, regardless of their actual condition. The nature of the Love Motif is embedded in that quality of being totally comfortable with every aspect of another person. Our level of comfort rises while striving to be fully present with them; the Love Motif is a desire to be a source of good, and to impact another person's life in a positive way.

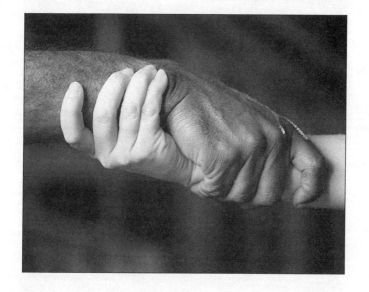

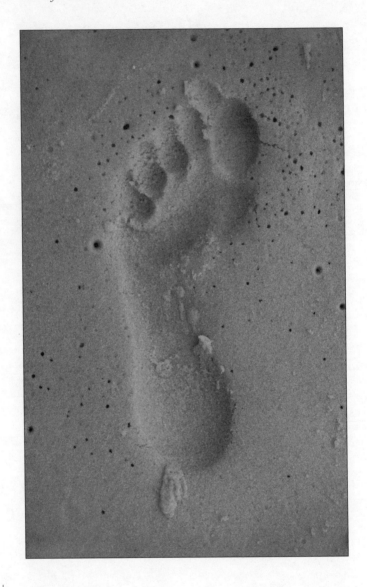

When working with clients, I try to discover where they are, meet them there, and then walk with them until we reach mutually identified goals. My method is, "C'mon, it's a scavenger hunt, I wonder what we can discover together." In other words, I want to be a companion on their journey.

I try to see the other person for who he or she is even though, at the outset, it may not be completely clear. It's for people to understand the importance of such an orientation in their interactions with others in their families, their workplaces, and their communities.

With many of the people I work with, it is as if they have been stamped with failure. So I try to sense the good qualities within these people and get them to express those qualities. And they say, "Yeah, I do see them—that's the way I am most of the time." But, they didn't ordinarily see those good qualities, because they lived with the image of failure that was projected onto them by others—they lived out that expectation of failing, rather than succeeding.

How do I know that people accept the values assigned to them by others? I use the same intuition that every person possesses to some degree. It's just a question of whether they use it and develop it. In my case, as I developed my own intuition, talents emerged that enabled me to recognize how a student or professional viewed their own self worth.

For example, early in my career, I observed that negativity often became overpowering in the minds of some students that had been referred to me. They would more readily absorb an "F" on their report card than recognize their own inherent positive qualities. They would become that F, blinded by negativity and oblivious to their own potential for success. People often view the loss of a position, professional goal, or marital relationship in much the same way. Over and over again I see professionals seemingly in the wrong-fit work culture or outright misplaced in a particular occupation. They often receive less than shining performance evaluations, not reflective of their actual abilities. And they themselves become such evaluations, much like students become their report card, and often just as early in life and career.

How Do We Help People Recognize and Nurture Their Own Gifts?

First, we have to help a troubled person recognize their gifts, and then nourish them with education. For example, early on I took courses that would equip me to work in psychology and education. Those courses gave me a foundation, which I overlaid with experience, where I then applied the principles to which I refer in this book.

The future belongs to

those who believe in the beauty of their dreams.

Eleanor Roosevelt

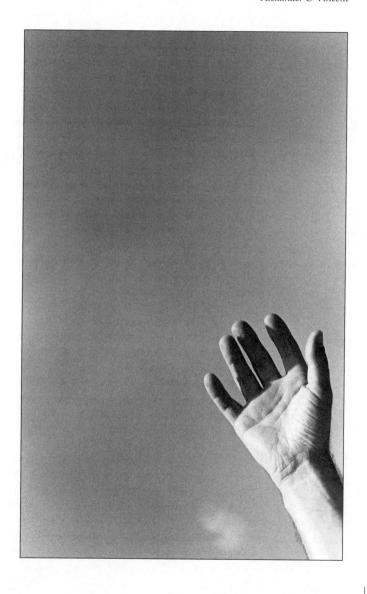

A side from my own success, there are a number of other approaches that we can develop and apply that play a role in the useful application of the Love Motif.

We all need to develop the ability to ask questions that cause another person to think about the gifts they do possess; questions that challenge them, and help them develop or reconsider what they believe. Furthermore, a person can be made aware that negative assumptions they make about themselves might contradict self-evident reality. Astute questioning on the part of the counselor has the effect of self-discovery on the part of the counseled, which further elevates the effect of negative assumptions.

I had a client who said, "God just made me that way and I can't read." It was then my place to ask, "Is that what you really believe?" That question gave them a moment and she responded, "No, Mrs. Alexander, I can't read just because I can't read." To which I responded, "Would you like to read?" "Well, yes," she said. Then we moved on to connecting at her level and starting from a place where she was most comfortable.

THE IMPORTANCE
OF PATIENCE

Patience happens bit-by-bit, and step-by-step. I try to be in sync with those I assist—not ahead of them or behind them. People must likewise develop and exercise patience in working with others in their own lives. It sounds simple, but it's so often overlooked—and it can provide a huge advantage to a person in need of counseling.

STILLNESS AND
THE LOVE MOTIF

Yeats described the experience of Stillness in his poem *The Celtic Twilight:*

We can make our minds so like still water that beings
gather about us that they may see,
it may be, their own images, and so live for a moment
with a clearer,
perhaps even with a fiercer life because of our quiet.

W. B. Yeats.

The connection between the Love Motif and the importance of Stillness allows us to become so still within ourselves that others are attracted to us because of our quiet. They can see themselves most clearly when in the presence of our stillness.

To get to a place of stillness, you need to have a one-on-one, fully present relationship with another person. You must be so attuned to the other human being from a place of your own quietness—being vitally interested in the other person. And they must feel instinctively that you believe in them. Patience and being in sync allows this level of trust and belief to occur.

THE WAY TO STILLNESS

Our clients need to find the still, small voice within them, wherever they happen to be. They should try to be silent for five minutes, to just *be*, and try to learn about themselves, to breathe deeply, and go to a safe place, to be aware of their environment and aware of the physical sensations in their body—relaxing each muscle group. Once clients have managed to meditate in this way, they say, "When can I come back and try climbing this hill again?"

I will tell you what my Way to Stillness has been. When I awake each morning, I breathe in the new day. I imagine God's love flowing into and all around me. I literally saturate myself in this love. Sometimes, I remember a dream I've had during the night and I try to recapture as much of that dream as I can on paper. Often, it is just a portion, but I find that if I remain focused on it, the entire dream will eventually surface.

At bedtime, I open myself to the possibility that whatever dreams I have, that may be significant in my life, will remain fresh in my mind. Next, I seek to allow an image to float into my consciousness and, pen in hand, try to jot down notes. I often find that I can recall the entire dream once I commit my memories to paper.

Each morning, I read something of meaning that I set out the night before. It may be a poem or a portion of a book, for instance, but it must affirm the presence of goodness, nearness, and healing power. It's about practicing to be in the presence of a power greater than ourselves.

In addition, I take a few minutes early in the morning to mentally name the task or the people to be helped. For me, I think about each of my clients for that day, knowing that love will go before both them and me. I see love as already having touched the experiences to come. This can be done while driving to work, traveling on the subway, fixing breakfast, or listening to an iPod. It's practical and portable.

STEPS TO STILLNESS
THROUGHOUT THE DAY

As I approach a difficulty or problem, at work or at home, I visualize a healing light enfolding me like a cloak. I relax my muscles and ask myself what it is I am feeling at that particular moment. I then try to name that feeling, whether it is anxiety, confusion, anger, or inadequacy. Once I identify it, I can embrace it with compassion, and then let it go.

As I approach others, face-to-face, by letter, by phone, or by computer, I visualize a presence of warmth and safety surrounding that person. I then look for a special uniqueness or beauty within them—trusting in my mind and heart that they will be helped to demonstrate those qualities more in their lives.

Thoughtful contemplation is important, too. And at some point in the day, I focus on a tree, a flower, a bird, a ray of sunshine and look at it fully and lovingly. If I can, I try to actually touch it physically or mentally and allow its beauty to emerge. I try to look within it, grateful for the comfort it brings.

At bedtime, I breathe quietly and visualize a relaxing, nurturing light flowing through my body. I gently touch on what has brought me pain, joy, or confusion during the day, and let it go. I also visualize anyone I met during the day who has special needs as being loved and protected.

DEPTH AWARENESS

The next Path to Stillness is Depth Awareness, which is a kind of recognition of a power greater than ourselves. This may require a leap of faith. It is the learning of how to say "yes" to the presence of God in our lives— daring to enter a deepening dialogue with a guiding presence. And, as we increasingly learn to say "yes" to this presence, we become revitalized with energy.

Even our bodies begin to change along with our attitudes. Some physicians have actually suggested that meditation and prayer generally, not from any particular denominational perspective, can lower blood pressure and reduce the heart rate. Herbert Benson MD of Harvard Medical School, author of *The Relaxation Response* and *Timeless Healing*, cites important studies that suggest patients with a variety of ailments respond positively to meditation and prayer. Patients with cancer, cardiac arrhythmia, chronic pain, and those recovering from open-heart surgery, as well as individuals suffering from depression and anxiety, have experienced a significant decrease in symptoms as well as a reduced recovery time. *New York Times* bestselling author Larry Dossey has also written extensively about the relationship between meditation and prayer and their powerful effects on physical and mental well-being and recovery time. His books, *Healing Words: The Power of Prayer and the Practice of Medicine* and *Prayer is Good Medicine* are considered to be pioneering texts in the field of spiritual healing.

Through the years I have watched hundreds of clients become more aware in this way. With each of them, their painful memories would begin to heal as awareness increased, and their defenses would begin to fall away.

When a client comes in, I have them sit quietly, trying to be aware of where their body feels stress or is uncomfortable. I have them imagine a warm, golden light surrounding their entire body, and ask them to breathe in that light. I ask them to try to imagine the golden light flowing through the top of their head, and slowly through their entire body—healing areas of pain. With each breath taken, the light penetrates deeper and deeper into the body.

I suggest they give thanks that their every cell is being filled with healing and that every breath is taking in spiritual nourishment. I have them repeat silently to themselves a verse or quotation that is meaningful to them, and to choose a mental image that helps them focus on an all-embracing love. I remind them to not strain for any special feeling, but rather to just rest quietly.

COMPASSIONATE AWARENESS

Compassionate awareness is another component of stillness. Compassionate awareness has more to do with applying a merciful understanding and sympathetic feeling to our past and to ourselves. I advise people to envision themselves as surrounded by a healing compassion and ask them to look honestly and directly at their feelings, including those brought on by any problems or difficult circumstances they may be facing. In addition, I suggest that they listen to each feeling as if it were a child who is hurt, troubled, or frightened. And finally, I encourage people to hold these feelings in a healing light.

I ask them to think of a memory that still hurts and then to go to that moment of pain or fear and invite this understanding energy to touch and heal it. I suggest that they allow the healing spirit to enter fully into the depths of their being—expressing a willingness for new energy and new gifts to be born within them.

I believe we cannot fully embrace the Love Motif without stillness in our souls. The extent to which one can move toward stillness is the extent to which one is in a place where they can truly listen, truly hear, and truly respond to the important stated or unstated needs of themselves or others.

Love is when we respond unconditionally to another person in a way that is prompted by their needs. This kind of response can easily become an automatic part of our interactions with others. It doesn't derive from organized religion. It isn't a platform from any particular denomination. We are given love to use for a particular place in our life, be it rising to a challenge or finding a path. You have to listen for it. In my life, it has been this way; my faith has been my constant throughout. Others may look to their faiths for similar consolation and guidance—it's really about living the Love Motif, seeing the Love Motif, being aware of the Love Motif, and expressing the Love Motif to all of humanity through our personalities and the gifts that we possess.

People often come to us feeling overwhelmed by the many challenges life is presenting—to the point that it's difficult for them to see love or experience love in their life, even to the point that they might lose sight of who they are and what matters most to them. But awareness of the talents and gifts that we have is so important, even if it begins with just a fascination for how the grass grows. It is therefore critical to provide these people with the best possible opportunity to learn their own talents and gifts.

Often real stimulation for learning comes in unexpected moments and in unexpected places. I wasn't necessarily out to do anything in particular for a client, such as giving them a learning device or a lecture. I was just there, present with them, on their own terms.

At the outset there might simply be a frustrated response, such as "I'm not interested in anything at all." But with a little prompting we would usually identify a particular interest or set of interests. At that point it would be up to me to help them discover, define, and develop that interest or set of interests.

The discovery of one's own gifts requires a healthy self-love. And that can be a process of discovery that requires patience, inner listening, and time for reflection.

Selections from First Corinthians 13—
New International Version, verses 4,5,6,7,13.

Love is patient, love is kind. It does not envy, it does not boast., it is not proud. It is not rude, it is not self-seeking, it is not easily angered, it keeps no record of wrongs. Love does not delight in evil but rejoices with the truth. It always protects, always trusts, always hopes, always perseveres. And now these three remain: faith, hope, and love. But the greatest of these is love.

Love is what is most important in this world and within us. The only thing that is enduring is love. Things sown in love, end in love. Things sown in fear, end in fear. We can do many things that are good. We can pursue a degree or do what it takes to be accomplished in a profession—whatever it may be—but unless it's prompted by love, which is intangible, then it amounts to nothing.

Our work with others is about wanting the best for the person with whom we are working. We work so that people may discover their gifts for themselves, and beyond that, for others in their lives, and so on.

We know we are being prompted when we feel guidance that seemingly comes from nowhere. It's a gut feeling—an intuition—it's a nudge ahead in one's thinking. We are also prompted by the synchronicity among others and us, which validates our intuition. Someone may say something that may cause you to reevaluate yourself or your relationships. A commercial on television might do the same, or the closing line of a letter, or something you read in a book. Who can say why you picked up that book, but we believe there was a reason.

This kind of awareness and the discernment that it makes possible is very rare in this world.

I've had physicians, attorneys, and business leaders who needed a bit of reminding about the importance of awareness. I will often ask them, "What can you tell me about Gandhi? What do you know about him?" When they reflect about it quietly for a moment, they have no problem identifying qualities that they valued in Gandhi's character like selflessness, courage, and compassion. They can usually identify particular aspects of his life in which the Love Motif was expressed in a manner they valued. As they did, they began to understand how it could be better expressed in their own lives.

Compassion, mercy, and peacemaking are all important gifts that make one a full person. We fall short without that indescribable motif as a compass in our lives, our true north.

To find that true north in your life, it is important to listen for your calling. Where do you fit within the structure of the world? Where can you make the most positive difference? How does your calling best serve the world? If one employs the Love Motif in their individual life it must not be kept isolated and serve only one's own narrow purposes. It must spill out into the world.

UNCONDITIONAL LOVE

Wise people know what time it is in their life; they look into their own heart and say, "If there be joy, it will be found within." They can be lit from within with their own wisdom.

Sometimes, it may take an act of will to avoid becoming closed to the Love Motif. This idea can be found throughout one of the books of the New Testament, in the book of John. John is infused with examples of unconditional love. In my own meditative and reflective life, I have found clues in the book of John regarding the mystery of divine love. For example, the story of the Samaritan woman in the fourth chapter of the Book of John is all about unconditional love.

In the story, Jesus sat down by a well to rest while his disciples went to locate food. A Samaritan woman came to draw water, and Jesus asked her for a drink. She turned to Him in surprise since Jews were not supposed to speak with those of her religion which was considered to be a corrupt form of the Jewish faith. "You are a Jew," she says, "and I am a Samaritan. Why ask me for water?" Jesus smiled at her and said "If you knew what God is able to give, or who it is that asks you for a drink, you would have asked Me to give you living water!" She then pointed out that he has no jug and that the well is deep. "How can you give me this living water?" Referring to the well water, Jesus said, "All who drink this water will thirst again, but whoever drinks my water won't thirst. My water flows like a fountain, giving eternal life." Now that Jesus had the woman's interest, she really wanted some of this water! Jesus looked deeply into her soul and told her things He could not have known about her troubled and unstable life unless, as she said, "He was a prophet!" She had had five husbands and her current live-in was

not her husband. In that time and culture, her colorful relationship history would have been termed "sinful" and wrong. What we might say today is that she had problems of relationship and maintaining connection. "Whoever drinks of the water that I shall give him will never thirst. But the water that I shall give him will become in him a fountain of water springing up into everlasting life." Jesus' complete acceptance and lack of judgment constitutes unconditional love. His goal was to present the message of eternal life to her with no strings attached.

Helping others through the Love Motif is about the lure of the irresistible enchantment and magnetism of unconditional love. In a universal sense, the condition of human alienation as exemplified by the Samaritan woman can be personalized within us. When we thirst for meaning, significance, and understanding, we must trust the Love Motif when and if another person is capable of totally accepting us. It doesn't matter what time it is in a person's life, there is always hope. It's never too late to experience unconditional love.

Total unconditional acceptance of each person as a unique human being should underlie our approach to those we counsel, in terms of who they are and what they may need, and it should underlie the nature of our relations with others. As a counselor, it has always been important to ask myself this question: *What is the true need of the person in this situation at this time?* The answer would take the focus off of me and put it onto the other person or situation. It was a way of matching my services to the needs of the person being counseled. I would then be able to take an honest and realistic self-appraisal and ask, "Is that something I can really provide?"

It's important to block out or distance ourselves from all the voices in the world that distract us—they tell us so many different things and cause us to lose our center. It is so important to draw oneself aside, on a daily basis, in the interest of one's own spiritual fitness in order to get to a place of stillness.

Getting to stillness can be helpful when people are in the midst of making an important decision and if they believe they've exhausted their options, or are confused about what they see ahead in their lives.

I believe we are prompted into stillness in our hearts and our minds, and the harmony that ensues. If one senses a disconnect it is not that a spiritual presence has ceased to be—it is simply that one lacks sufficient stillness. In order to benefit fully, one has only to draw aside and be in the right place, to be open to it.

DREAMS

reams can be helpful to us in clarifying aspects of our life. My daughter told me of a dream she had twenty years ago in which she observed me in a room underneath the city of Jerusalem, sitting at a wooden table with Christ. I was all alone in a foreign land, and yet my life intersected with this presence of great love. She described the amazing unconditional love emanating from this robed man and his patience with my difficulty in articulating words. The words I was using were not even in my language—they came from a place deep inside me—and yet, I recognized them as belonging to this man—they were his name. In her dream, I also sensed that he was my only hope of finding my way home.

My daughter describes me as having a speech impediment in the dream, as though my mouth was full of marbles. I struggled to say the words, "Yeshua Hamishia" to this man. Months after her dream, she learned from a biblical scholar that, in the dream, I was calling the robed man the Messiah in the Aramaic language.

The way I interpreted the dream is that God recognizes love in us and we recognize the same in him. As in the dream, I struggle to identify him and my speech is garbled. God recognizes any and all attempts to approach him. The dream was synchronous in that it supplied words that in real life neither my daughter nor I knew.

I see myself in that dream as though I were the Samaritan woman encountering the robed man for the first time—bringing my brokenness before him. When I hear my daughter relate this dream, as I imagine that scene, I can feel the presence of unconditional love emanating from this man. My best attempts to address him by name fell short, just as the woman at the well was unable to identify this man until he had told her so much about herself, and in so doing his divinity was revealed.

Just as it did in the Samaritan woman's story, the recognition of unconditional love can give us renewed meaning and purpose for our lives knowing that there is some higher power that wills goodness for all of us. That understanding can prompt us to try to find ways to channel the recognition of love into the lives of others.

PURPOSE

My work in counseling individuals provides tremendous experiences in and of itself. I can't imagine any kind of investment in one's life that could provide more of a return. Is this how an engineer feels after designing a bridge or edifice and seeing it come to completion? The principle of attraction over promotion may explain why individuals who are in need of counseling are drawn to it by the force of the Love Motif.

The Love Motif guarantees that the under and over purpose (over purpose meaning the general big picture/mission statement and the under purpose meaning the more specific, day-to-day one) for our lives will be correct because it is God-given. I want so much for others. Each of us has to find what it is that we serve in our hearts and with our minds. Regardless of the mistakes I may make every day, my counseling is an expression of love when I honestly try to use the Love Motif.

Although I never felt the need to market my work, marketing itself can actually be an extension of the Love Motif. For whatever reason, the Love Motif has worked for me. It allows others to be aware of what we have to offer them.

A Spiritual Connection

Therefore, I am now going to allure her. I will lead her into the desert and speak tenderly to her. There I will give her back her vineyards, and make the valley of trouble a door of hope. *Hosea 2:14 — 15*

How do you check on your emotional or spiritual state each day? For me, it's not just by getting to stillness, but also by recognizing that there exists a power greater than myself. In the last several years I have had that recognition when I wake up in the morning. It is not like seeing something, religiously inspired or otherwise, but it is in being so possessed with his love that it may come out in laughter or in another surprising fashion. Yet it isn't anything I am able to put on or take off like a sweater. And it's fun—life is really fun with that kind of a spiritual connection. Having such a robust spiritual connection doesn't mean that I haven't gone through very difficult times, but in such times that spiritual connection is essential. It helped me through the loss of my husband, Dave,

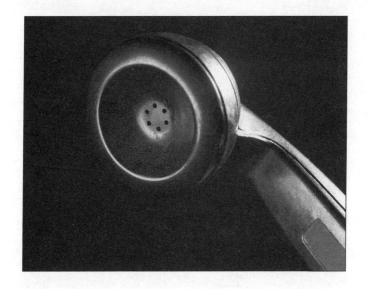

and the loss of my mother, who was a very important force in my life. Just knowing they weren't here on earth anymore, and that I was no longer able to experience their presence was a source of discomfort. But there were also joyous times—the birth of each of my girls. I've been able to recall the emotions and feelings I experienced when I woke up in the hospital with each one. I distinctly remember, even prior to discovering their genders, waking up and saying, "Thank you, Father, thank you again for another child."

Practicing the discipline of gratitude at times of great joy as well as loss is a good way to check on and maintain one's spiritual fitness and balance. I have clients who, at the end of each day, write down at least three things for which they are grateful. In this way I am trying to help them to establish a spiritual connection that will help them find a way to stillness.

BEING RIGHT-MINDED

The story of the Samaritan woman has really been a touchstone for me throughout my life.

The core and universal concept associated with the Samaritan woman that most resonates with me is that she had a huge hunger in her soul and was offered God's love, which could fill her completely. There is hunger in the soul, the heart, and the life of everyone, which is a yearning for "right-mindedness," and I believe this is essentially the same as the Love Motif.

Right-minded means having access to a spiritual connection, access to the divine. Although every individual may not know what to call it, there is a hole in their heart and until that's filled with a healthy love, they are not whole. Therefore, it is essential to the spiritual health of each person to consider how they can become more right-minded, in order to fill that hole with healthy love.

The peace that comes into the heart of a person as a result of their search for right-mindedness is beyond description. It is definitely one of the most important things for a client to embrace, because it imbues one's perspective with the recognition of what is outside of and greater than oneself. It also allows an understanding of its relationship to what lies uniquely within oneself. People are thirsty for such understanding. The thirst of the Samaritan woman at the well went far beyond the physical need for water—it was a spiritual need for right-mindedness.

COUNSELOR-CLIENT DIFFERENCES

I come from a Christian belief system that has guided my life and which has influenced aspects of my approach to counseling and guidance to others. Yet, the range of clients I have advised over the years encompasses people, young and old, from diverse cultural and religious backgrounds. And because those clients have represented so many backgrounds and belief systems other than my own, one might wonder how I advise those whose beliefs may be very different from mine. The question must be: what is the best way to provide service when our first inclination is to draw on our own faith, and when our client does not share our faith?

PSALM XXIII.

David's confidence in God's grace.

A Psalm of David.

THE LORD *is* ^amy shepherd; ^bI shall not

2 ^cHe maketh me to lie down in † green

adeth me beside the † still waters.

He restoreth my soul: ^ehe leadeth me in

teousness for his name's sake.

ea, though I walk through the valley of 'the

^gI will fear no evil: ^hfor thou *art wit*

ff they comfort me.

ou preparest a tabl

thou †

Helping those with different beliefs does not have to be difficult. It has to do with the nature and quality of deep listening and complete acceptance of and respect for another person, regardless of the background from which they come, or the beliefs they may hold. It's about reciprocity between one human being and another—not one above or over another. It is the connection between one soul to another. It's about being genuinely excited about them in terms of their potential. It is about mutual respect, and most clients have no problem realizing that. It's about being comfortable with silence and allowing silence to bridge differences. All of these factors enhance the quality and clarity of a client's thoughts and feelings. As a result, what often happens is that clients see things, understand things, and see solutions that would otherwise not have been apparent.

The ministry I am describing is one of presence—a kind of common denominator in human relations. In my experience, the qualities we are talking about make for rich communication with others, regardless of orientation or denomination.

The Love Motif levels the ground where we stand and allows us to stand together. Love always levels the ground on which we stand. For as long as I have been practicing, my heart's prayer has been to be fully present for a client, and to clarify and respond to the deepest needs of that client. That is the absolute bedrock of my practice.

HOPE

The world stands out on either side

No wider than the heart is wide;

Above the world is stretched the sky,

No higher than the soul is high.

The heart can push the sea and land

Farther away on either hand;

The Soul can split the sky in two,

And let the face of God shine through.

—Edna St. Vincent Millay

excerpt from *Renascence*

This poem has always been a message of hope for me. It stands for a world of inspiration as we stumble along in our lives, and there's such spiritual power in its message. It reminds me of my efforts to help with the intellectual and spiritual search of all the international students I had the good fortune to meet with and become close to at Vanderbilt University's Peabody College for Teachers.

Vanderbilt was one of the first universities to initiate programs that brought international students to the states in large numbers. Somehow these students from such wide-ranging cultural and religious backgrounds found their way to our home, and some ended up living there.

The seeming distances and vast cultural differences among those students vanished as my husband, David, and I opened our hearts and our home to each of them. I believe that they gravitated to us because we were more about being a welcoming presence than about doctrine. We were more about love than particular religious beliefs. Love and acceptance, flowing through us, leveled the common ground on which we were standing.

THE DIFFERENT KINDS OF LOVE

There are different classifications of love, and I tend to use the Greek classification, just as the members of the early Church did: Agape, which refers to God's unconditional love for us; Eros, which refers to romantic and sexual love; and Philia, which refers to brotherly love and a unity among human beings.

There are, however, other ways of categorizing love. I make a distinction between "gift love," which at its best is a love that gives and expects nothing in return, and "need love," which still gives but only with the expectation of a reward. The difference between the two really hinges on reciprocity.

Taking a client on simply for the amount of exchange, i.e. the money, the fee, or even to be provided with meaningful work, is participating in need love. In the case of need love, the expectation of a reward is a primary concern, without which a service would not be rendered. It would be difficult for me to be in that position and still

consider it love, but human frailties being what they are, it is possible.

Gift love might best be described as being fully present to another with the totality of my life. It's about what we can give, regardless of what may or may not be received. There is no thought for ourselves or about what we can get out of a relationship. Gift love occurs when I feel where the other person is and I am there, fully present, despite all my frailties. This ability to be present occurs as I posture myself and align my will, in a selfless way, with divine will. This is actually an essential part of how I begin each morning, no matter what must be faced in the course of the day to come. Gift love, so described, is the mission and goal of my life and work.

If I may, I would like to share the words of my late good friend, theologian, and author John Claypool, on the gift love vs. need love distinction.

"It is the old dichotomy between need love and gift love that C.S. Lewis talks about. He said 'need love' is essentially self-serving—there is an emptiness in me that attempts to be filled at the expense of another. Thus, I go forth in love to an object, not in order to give something of myself, but to get something for myself. My love moves out for the purposes of extracting something of value and bringing it back to me. This is at bottom an acquisitive process, similar to the way a vacuum in nature sucks everything back into its own emptiness."

Claypool goes on to describe gift love as "a fullness that is willing to spin itself in behalf of the beloved." It is not a circle going out to come back, but simply an arc. Its great desire is the transfer of value from subject to object, not the other way around. It wants only to enhance and enrich the other, not to extract or exploit.

When I am in touch with the source of all love, I am renewed, and my capacity to extend gift love to others is enriched. Gift love existed in my work, and I think it also existed with the girls and with Dave, when we responded to the needs of others, audible and inaudible, with no thought of return.

In the depth of winter, I finally learned

that within me there lay

an invincible summer.

—Albert Camus

How to Recognize Needs in Others

Each morning, in silent prayer, I ask that I be able to recognize the needs of others. I make it a point to get up early for my counseling practice to ensure that I have some quiet time to think about the needs of those with whom I would be meeting that day. I am amazed at what occurs afterward.

When, for instance, two people are in a relationship, it might be the case that one or both partners could love out of a sense or feeling of need for the other person. Alternatively, one or both might love more on the basis of wanting to give a gift to the other. I believe that, for longer than I can remember, this distinction has perfectly described important relationships in my life. I loved Dave, and obviously there were needs met. It was the romantic kind of love, but it was the closest thing to that unconditional, perfect love that I have ever experienced. That, of course, doesn't mean there weren't ups and downs of marriage, but it buoyed our relationship and allowed us to deal with the hard times.

As far as my girls are concerned, I loved them completely and without conditions. When they were teenagers, they did everything I could imagine to try my patience. As angry as I could become for their behavior, it never altered my feeling of real love for each of them.

As for my work, when there were successes, the use of the Love Motif was a matter of instinct. No matter what people brought in terms of emotional baggage or regrets, I believe it was my total acceptance of who they were that played the most important role in my successful efforts with them. I didn't have to manufacture concern or compassion—I truly embraced an unconditional acceptance of that other person.

Agape love makes and molds our response to the human predicament. We think and sometimes say, "Wow, thank you, Father, you did this, I could never have done it." Sometimes it's in my own best interest, or it makes me feel good. Sometimes, all I can do is offer a prayer of thanksgiving. If I can offer such a prayer, then I'm doing my best in this partnership that I have with God.

In all those years of working with students and professionals, I depended on a spiritual connection. I consider it a miracle, and it took my humanity plus God to create it. When a client would say that a miracle had happened, it was something I had always already known. It was the spiritual connection between Gayle Alexander and the client, and that never dimmed.

I believe that the quiet time I spent at my desk each morning, saturating my thoughts with the needs of the day's clients, was extraordinarily helpful to the quality of the connection I was able to establish with them. This was the primary means by which I created the basis for accessing and engaging other people on such a deep level. I recommend that everyone confronted with any similar task do the same. What is wonderful is that my ability to engage clients in this way seems to have come more easily with age.

I believe that without a spiritual source of power it would not have been possible to do the kind of work that I do. The Love Motif has sustained me throughout my career, despite all of my shortcomings, frailties, and lack of knowledge. Without the Love Motif, I would not have found success.

THE TRUEST LOVE

Each day, when I first open my eyes, I pray a prayer of gratitude for another day and ask that God's will be present in all I do and say. How much more we can experience the Love Motif in our lives when we allow ourselves to feel the fresh touch of a loving presence each morning! This is what I consider to be the Truest Love. Truest Love is the purest, most authentic and genuine love.

In order for people to find the truest love, it is important to go back to the steps to stillness. In doing so, they can put themselves in a place that enables them to best identify what qualities they most appreciate and value. It is extremely personal.

I have often been asked to offer guidance to someone in a relationship who seems to be motivated out of need for the other person, rather than being motivated to give a gift of love to them. I have to remember that there are aspects of each type of love in the best of relationships, so I try to lead them to understand the difference between the two types of love. I feel as if I am holding a mirror for them to see what they've been emphasizing in life. I encourage a person to understand their motives for first entering and then maintaining the relationship. At some point in that discussion, I simply ask point blank whether they are motivated to obtain something from their partner, or to enrich the life of their partner.

Relationships involve both types of love, as has been the case in my own life. I would love to think that everything is perfect and my relationships are the epitome of agape. But I have the sense to accept my own imperfections, as we all need to, before we can come closer to achieving the unconditional acceptance of others. Self-acceptance has to happen first, and then one can most fully extend it to others. When self-acceptance is healthy enough, our instincts and our power to meet others via the Love Motif are enhanced. We stay within the relationship itself, and we are able to avoid projecting our own beliefs regarding, for example, faith, politics, or economics, onto other people. We move into a state of philia love, in which we accept each other as we are regardless of human imperfections.

Gift love involves the feeling of being with someone with no regard for what they might be doing, even if they are engaged in despicable or criminal activities. It is strong enough to love them through anything, and the sense of yearning to be with them springs from human empathy.

Divine gift love is God wanting the best for all of us, and providing for us no matter what. The guidance we need is there simply for the asking, and by asking we create a relationship with something larger than ourselves. I've tried to share the life that is made possible for us by applying the Love Motif in my work. We are guided, directly or indirectly, through grave and horrible things, and we know we couldn't make it without that divine recognition. We're all being guided no matter where we are, through times of tears and times of joy.

DIVINE DIRECTION

Whatever places I have found myself in, I have prayed for a sense of divine presence—and what relief I have experienced when I have done so. A simple prayer can bring a guiding presence far greater than ourselves into our consciousness, especially in times of personal tragedy and disaster.

It is fair to ask how one knows whether he or she is receiving direction from a divine guiding presence, or receiving it from someplace else. For me, it is the strong and lucid sense of recognition of God within my mind and heart. For example, remember Mike and Mr. Brierson, the boiler man? I felt that I was divinely guided to ask Mike if he would like to see that machinery, and to ask Mr. Brierson for permission to enter the restricted access boiler room on behalf of this young boy's urgent interest. We had the chance to change that boy's life, and because of a divinely inspired guiding presence, it was changed. Mr. Brierson explained the machines, diagrams, and workings of the equipment and fixtures, and that was all that Mike needed. Many people asked me, "How could you do that? How could you go to those extremes?" To me, it wasn't extreme, just basic and obvious. I couldn't *not* do it.

Again, the equation was God plus Mike plus me equals success. The man pulling those great doors of the boiler room back—Mr. Brierson—gave Mike a booklet about the workings of the boiler room, all tattered and torn, that Mike put into his back pocket. I told Mike that some day he would be able to read it.

It is important to realize that my mental and physical natures needed to be in sync with each other and with Mike. I prayed earlier that I would be given these ideas and the energy to perfect them. The fact is, these things that took place around the boiler room were miracles, as were the subsequent removal of the blocks so Mike could read.

There is one other element of this divinely directed success that was critical. The cooperation of people on many different levels was amazing. As I would attempt to jot down the names of people that had a part in making

this possible, I realized that it was too many people for it to have been an accident. No chance for a coincidence. We have access to people we would not otherwise have access to through divine guidance.

SEX AND LOVE

In cultures such as ours where so much emphasis is placed on sex, I have always thought of sexual love—Eros—as a gift from God. Eros is a sacred gift to be offered to one's beloved. Ultimately, whether a person is expressing himself or herself sexually in a healthy way is between that person and God, which is another way of saying that what's important is that people be at peace with themselves. We are sexual beings and each person must find the most appropriate place in their life to best express their own sexual gifts. However, I am not suggesting that there be any boundary violations of the loyalties associated with a committed relationship.

CHARACTER AND COURAGE

There is a guiding presence with us, even when we do not recognize it. We simply have to get to a point of stillness to be aware of it. People become so exhausted expending their efforts fruitlessly that, deep down, they may not be conscious of what is right in front of them. A presence, or perhaps the opportunity offered by that presence, may come in many forms. Such an opportunity can help a person through a difficult situation and on to the next step. From that step there is usually an opening for the next step, which we can take on faith.

Character makes unconditional love possible. It serves as both a foundation and a filter for our values and our choices, and allows us to offer love to ourselves and to others. In my work, I always strive to love unconditionally. That doesn't mean that I don't need to place limits on my time and energy in particular situations; I do because it is necessary to protect my own well being, and allows me to continue to be an effective instrument in service to others. Sometimes the best way to love others is to protect myself from being exploited.

It can be difficult to differentiate between character and courage. There are many different kinds of courage, and one of them is believing in someone when they don't believe in themselves. That may not be what one thinks of as courage, but without that, I wouldn't be in the line of work I am in. Unless I believe that there's more than what meets the eye in a particular person—and that includes brainpower—I would never have seen them twice. Often the record that accompanies a client and the evidence arrayed against them had pointed to failure in many different ways—in grades, in disposition, in the whole person, in past judgments and in life decisions. But being able to see in them what they don't see themselves is a crucial step to helping them achieve their potential as a human being.

It would be useful for each of us to develop our own ability to see the qualities in ourselves of which we may not be aware. It takes the grace of God —that's capital G, Grace—to know that there's more than just a teacher, or a

parent, or whoever inside me, even though I don't see it myself. There is a sense, however, that there are internal reserves there that haven't been tapped, and that same sense is there within everybody. I believe in that sense enough to be able to walk with my clients, not in front of them, and not behind them, but alongside them until they achieve their goal.

Courage for me is to submerge myself into a client's circumstances and be willing to be drowned, wiped out, and obliterated by them. My goal is to get that other person to be in touch with at least what I thought was there for them. Reaching that goal is the height of success, and it's worth my life's efforts. It is often difficult, often scary, but I keep moving ahead, no matter what. I think that the divinely inspired grace, what I call "God givenness," is courage quite beyond humanity.

God givenness is a reference to the ideas being placed in my mind. They were there when I was given the idea to get the doors of the boiler room open on a Saturday morning, so the miracle of one boy being helped to read could occur.

The experience of the painful and unjust circumstances associated with the loss of my husband's unique and important position was just such an experience. And then, several days later, our home burned. Like most people when faced with a multitude of great challenges and losses, my first thought was, "I don't know what to do." Needless to say, there was a place for courage in such a situation. And it was courage, beyond what we thought was there, that got us through. Sometimes just acting as if you had the courage to go on is courage enough. Simply putting one foot in front of the other, doing the next thing that needs to be done, regardless of the circumstances, is most important. One also needs to have the willingness and courage to bring others on board to help. This constellation of relationships emboldens us by allowing us to experience the support of love from a number of people around us. In our practice, we have often brought in a variety of people to assist clients for this very reason.

The relationship between character and courage is vital. How can we have one without the other? Character in a

person allows them to acknowledge that there is something in them that enables them to keep going on and then to do something electrifying. Courage is when it looks like a door is closed, and one can walk towards it anyway. It may slam shut, but to keep walking towards that door, not knowing whether it's going to open, is courage.

WORK AND MISSION

I have been blessed to work with an accomplished group of people that has included physicians, attorneys, members of the clergy, and business leaders. For instance, while just out of college and counseling students at a youth center, I worked and lived with a well-off family headed by a captain of industry. As is the case with most families and organizations, the individual family members had relationship problems. Each of them was very eager to have someone listen to them person to person, and to really hear and experience them beyond the confines of their tremendous estate. Persons of great material wealth are often the most in need of this kind of counseling.

At the family estate, where the corporate headquarters were, I sat with lawyers and business people who were confronted with challenging circumstances, and was able to counsel them. I don't know if I was ever more effective than I was at that time, even after all of these years. It

was meeting after meeting, attorney after attorney, sitting with the family. Somehow I was able to draw the people together and assist them in resolving conflicts associated with decisions they were making. And I was only twenty-one years old!

This situation is similar to when couples involved in a divorce move toward litigation and the levels of anxiety and tension tend to escalate. Early on, I discovered that the mediation process we conducted in our beautiful retreat setting decreased those anxieties and, in many cases, got the relationship back on track. In the late 70s, we began to provide mediation services for couples and families on inheritance issues, for business pΔartners involved in financial and organizational disputes, and other forms of law related corporate conflicts and conduct. We looked for and often found creative solutions that worked out very well for all parties involved. The surprised lawyers would just say, "Wow, how did you get these people together?"

In my lectures on character and courage I talk about how I've been influenced by individuals whose contributions have spilled out into the world. The work of women whom I consider to be great souls, such as Mother Teresa, Queen Noor, and Madeleine Albright, embody many of the qualities I value most.

Then there is Ruth from the Old Testament. The account that we have in the Bible makes it crystal clear that she was true to her identity. She went against the conventions and traditions of the time by leaving the land of her birth to enter an unknown geographic territory and make that new land her home. Just as Ruth gathered grain in the fields daily, I consider my reading of the Old Testament and the New Testament as a daily harvest of spiritual food, for my life. This has been particularly affirming in my own life, as well as in the lives of the people I know.

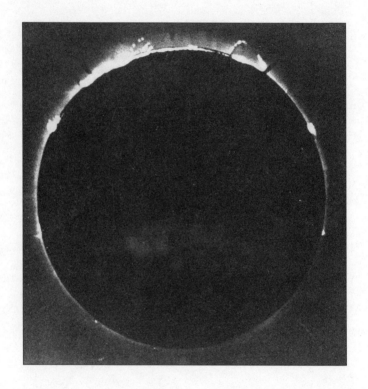

In terms of character and courage, Ruth modeled for us the idea that every person is responsible for connecting with their inner call, even if it may mean leaving behind the familiar in order to embrace change. She was willing to set herself apart from the broader culture and leave behind material comfort and security. Sticking to her vision of what was right for her, and maintaining her own integrity, enabled her to triumph over her fears—fears that any of us would have while making such a bold move.

The inspiration garnered from a reading of Ruth can be very encouraging in this year of natural disasters, famine, and global oppression. The desire to share deeply in the lives of others in whatever ways their hunger seems to express itself is critical, as opposed to superimposing our own desired outcomes. Any way a person might wish to open up and receive counseling is valid, and the more committed they are to their own integrity and vision, the better. I make myself available, on those terms, to those who approach me for counseling and personal direction.

My husband, Dave, interviewed Mother Teresa early in his career while working globally to provide spiritual counseling to young people. He found her to be so open to the Holy Scriptures that she moved him to actively pursue a life of prayer. She gave him a kind of running account of how much prayer had meant in her life and admonished him as a young man to "look into that." He was amazed at how current she was in terms of the words she used and the ideas that she expressed. She accompanied him all along the streets of Calcutta as he visited different schools.

You can imagine how astonishing it was to a young university chaplain to be given that kind of experience by someone like Mother Teresa. She said to him "David, no matter how busy you get as a university chaplain, there's never anything as important as daily communication with the Holy One." He never forgot that, and it led him into a discipline of prayer that I think he would never have experienced otherwise.

Because of that early admonishment, David included a 4 a.m. early-morning prayer in his routine—an hour or two daily for the rest of his life. Doing so enabled him to face the adversity and challenges he would endure over the next fifty years. It was through a sense of Mother Teresa's presence that he was able to carry on his work as director of World Missions through university campuses in India and other countries. When he returned to the states, he never lost his sense of Mother Teresa's presence, or his discipline of daily prayer. Regardless of our situations, we can all impact the lives of others in positive and life altering ways.

As Dave traveled around the world, he remembered how deeply moved he had been by Mother Teresa. She gave her time and attention to people literally dwelling in the gutter, in the streets where they had gone, trying to help them. He recalled having been so tired, yet thinking that it wouldn't have stopped her from going on. I remember Dave quoting her, saying "There's still more to be done by humanity." By this she meant keep going forward, touching one person at a time, life by life.

Mother Teresa made a huge difference in just one person, my husband, which affected him for the rest of his life, and that is still amazing to me. I'm deeply grateful for it, because the influence she had on my life and work was incalculable as well.

The sustained courage it must have taken to tread those streets of Calcutta, daily ministering to people in the streets and gutters, wherever she found them, was remarkable. She used the phrase "in the presence" to describe the divine presence in her work. I remember Dave saying, "In the Presence always of The Holy One,"—which serves as a reminder that each of us can bring a part of this presence to the lives of those with whom we live and work.

SERVICE

Everyday acts of service and courage have to be prompted by the real thing, by love—they can't be counterfeited. In my own life, it seems I need that recognition of the divine day-after-day. I find it sustaining. Since my college years I have taken several minutes a day to pray silently, praying for whoever comes into my mind. Sometimes I have prayed for people whose names I didn't even know, but I could see their faces. I would just turn aside from all other activity and clear my mind and quiet my heart. In many cases, my guidance for others just comes up and out, and since it must have been engendered somehow, I would say it flows from the Love Motif.

In the five minutes before I put on my makeup and put on my things to go out into the world every day, I have quiet time to restore my spiritual connection. I ask for the divine to work through me, so that I may be of service to others.

It has been very natural for me to do this—my intention is not to exaggerate my experience. Using the Love Motif is not the same as putting on a garment every morning. Perhaps I'm needier than most people, who don't have to beseech God for the guidance it takes to live out love for others. But seeking divine guidance to gain stillness is a structure of my being that I feel very deeply—although it's difficult for me to express in words—this sustained love for others, all through the day.

SEASONS OF THE HEART

Seasons of the Heart refers to personal experiences I've had and recognition that the disappointments I've experienced may very well be seen as "his appointments." Changing one letter turns a negative into a divinely inspired challenge. This perspective has influenced the way I have dealt with different disappointments throughout life. I have had dry seasons interspersed with fertile seasons, just as everyone else does—it's all a part of life.

The Love Motif can be seen as a constant, however, kind of like the sun. It is always there, even as the weather changes, even if it isn't immediately visible. The perspective of the Love Motif allows me to see a seeming disappointment as an opportunity for success, being offered to me through my faith in God and it turns disappointment into His appointment.

It's been a great experience for me to see how many times disappointment could be converted into His appointment. It's often very difficult to accept disappointment, but the Love Motif has reminded me that a simple shift in perspective—changing one letter—is all it takes to give me a positive attitude. Throughout the years I have found this concept to be helpful to many people, from all walks of life.

Some thirty years ago on a European study opportunity, I had hoped to hear Viktor Frankl lecture in Vienna. Viktor Frankl was a respected physician and psychologist in Vienna, Austria, when he was taken to a concentration camp. He lost not only his family but also the impressive body of his life's work. He survived by projecting himself to the other side of his suffering by visualizing lectures he would be giving in the future about the experience. His strategy allowed a kind of rebirth. His wonderful book, *Man's Search for Meaning,* details his experience and serves to remind people of the possibility of transcending their difficult experiences, appropriating crises and suffering, and finding meaning in these experiences. I was, naturally, disappointed when, upon arriving at the lecture site, I was informed that, the lecture had to be canceled due to an emergency.

Frankl's book, *Man's Search for Meaning*, had a profound effect on my life. I was so moved that I did something I had never done before: I wrote him two or three lines of appreciation for the book. In response to my note, he sent a postcard with a picture of his cat on it and expressed his gratitude for what I had said in my note to him, which he said that he saved. He indicated that he had hoped to come to the United States, and he wondered if we might meet and compare notes. We continued a correspondence and came to know each other quite well through letters.

After a year or so, I was able to arrange for him to speak in Nashville. He indicated he would like to come and we could finally have that coffee together. Needless to say, the auditorium was packed and people were standing on the outside. It was a tremendous turnout and reception, and he was genuinely moved. The coffee date we had scheduled became a lunch date.

Frankl's main idea is that disappointment might better be viewed as an opportunity. If something doesn't work out initially, there may be a reason. The time that I was able to spend with Viktor Frankl really helped drive home these points, and the time we spent was such quality time—so much more than I could have initially expected—all because his Vienna lecture had been canceled— my disappointment.

When Frankl and I looked into each other's eyes there was complete peace, serenity, and a certain purity that I have gone back to as a refuge in times of crisis. It was a sense of presence that spoke volumes. We could stand without speaking and be fully present with each other—he knew I was truly with him, and I knew he was truly with me. He wrote the words "Soul meets soul," to describe our meeting and interaction. It was a spiritual presence, a "kinship"—as if we were both looking out on the world in the same direction and from the same perspective.

MIRACLE OF HEALING

Several years after my college graduation, I received a telephone call from the parents of my favorite roommate, whom I'll call Jenny. They indicated they had something to ask of me. Jenny had been in a deep coma for several weeks. The coma was such that she didn't appear to recognize anyone, even her physician.

I went to her bedside to join her mother and father, and there we stood. I said, "Jenny...?" I'm not sure there was any movement from her at all, and it seemed as if there was no recognition of my presence. But at that moment the doctor came back into the room, not having seen her for several days, and stepped up to her. She opened her eyes, looked up at him and said. "Doctor, you can make me well." It seems that somehow my presence did have some type of effect on her—it triggered something.

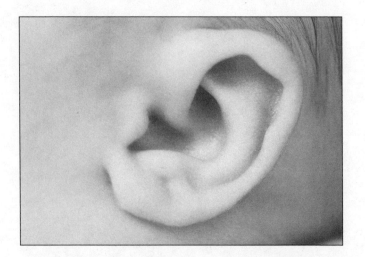

She may have regained consciousness by being prompted by the presence of someone who had meant so much to her. Our friendship was deep enough that it did not matter that we had not seen or corresponded with each other for several years. This experience of healing, this miracle, was brought about purely by friendship.

I believe in the sun,

Even when it is not shining.

I believe in Love,

Even when I feel it not.

I believe in God,

Even when he is silent.

Words found written on the walls of a cellar

in Cologne, Germany after WWII

LETTING GO OF RIGHT

I was visited, in my office, by a very stern father who had great expectations for each of his sons, who were also present. When one son inappropriately condemned the other's behavior, the father took him by the shoulders and said, "You are so full of what's right, that you can't see what's good." It behooves us to reflect on this principle of a higher law of love, even over protocol or propriety.

Sometimes we need to let go of our preconceived ideas of what is right—in the service of seeing what can be accomplished by a higher law of love. When a person or individual operates from the Love Motif and loves unconditionally, it allows the healing grace of God to come into a situation. This is an important point for all people to think about in their relations with others, because it can run counter to common sense, habit, or routine.

Sometimes people can be so preoccupied with a black and white sense of what is right, that they can only see what's wrong in someone else's behavior; in so doing, the good in that person's motivation for acting as they did can be missed. Sometimes one person's condemnation of another is nothing more than a need to be right—such condemnation is often a fear-based form of control. Throughout the years, I've been mindful of the father's lesson—I've taken myself by the shoulders when I have become aware of being in the mindset of the older brother in this situation, and shut my mouth when I might have said something I would later regret.

GRAVE CLOTHES

There are many disappointments and unrecognized opportunities in my life—those that have related to helping others and those that have related to my own growth. I call them my "grave clothes." In my work with people, I often ask them, "What are your grave clothes?"

When I think about the question of grave clothes, I look at my own humanness and the times when I have felt powerless, even within my own family, when I have been looked to by others for guidance. There were times when I wished I could have been the instrument in my own home that I had been for others in my professional life. It was these times, when I was trying so hard to hear the still small voice within, that I was unable to hear the voices of those nearest to me. I am so sorry for that.

I know that what I'm expressing is not at all uncommon, but all of my life I have wanted to be sure that I have taken responsibility for every opportunity to grow, both spiritually and socially. I've stumbled along, having missed many opportunities that I can't recapture. So I try to start each new day in prayer, saying "Father, I'm open to you and the opportunities you give me." That's my constant prayer of simply being. I don't have to give anything or do anything. I just am —and that's enough. And whatever I do is able to grow out of that attitude in my heart and in my mind.

Grave clothes is a reference to the folded linens that in many cultures were left in the tomb. But for me they symbolize traditions that are old and worn out—all the deadening things in our lives that continue to take us down, as opposed to those things that create new life within us. For example, I may be still clinging and responding to particular aspects of my past in the same old way, or I'm being unfairly critical of someone or something. In donning these grave clothes, I have missed opportunities simply to be. I find this happening when I strive to fix problems of other people who cannot or do not wish to be fixed. Instead of fighting against it and being drawn into a negative frame of mind, I have learned to just accept the situation and let it be.

Examples of Grave Clothes

Perfectionism and compulsive people pleasing. These are behavior patterns that can appear to look good to others, but in reality can be quite harmful by damaging integrity and avoiding the hard choices that are necessary for growth.

Lack of autonomy in our lives. Feeling that we have no freedom of choice.

Worry and anxiety. Unproductive fretting over those things we cannot control.

Selfishness. An unhealthy inwardness that restricts one's potential.

Being haunted by the past. Harboring negative experiences and feelings of resentment or regret.

Self-centered fear. Always thinking about how this would affect me.

Self-burdening. In the words of one client, holding the title of "Manager of the Universe and Beyond." This is simply the feeling that the weight of the world is on our shoulders, and we are responsible for everything in which we are involved.

Losing our true self in the Service of Service. Here, service can become a trap when one tends to overload oneself on behalf of others.

Loss of hope. Total inability to envision something positively better for oneself.

Addictions. Any area of our lives in which we have lost our power to make healthy choices.

These examples and other grave clothes represent common forms of self-destructive behavior that many people can relate to. They continue to "kill" us by murdering our soul, day in and day out. Daily spiritual discipline can be helpful in dealing with our grave clothes. We must be willing to persist in the face of defeat, and to exert our uniquely human energy to free ourselves. If someone wants it badly enough, it will happen, thanks to the potential of the miracle within. Of course, we should not always depend on the possibility of that miracle. Rather, we usually supply that miracle of freedom, through our own potential.

WHICH VOICE?

How can one best discern between the voices inspired by the universal presence I have described, versus other, distracting voices in times of important decision making? Stillness is the key. It is through stillness, through the reaching of an inner quiet, that one can get the clarity that allows for the richest thinking. Stillness requires daily discipline in order to be developed. It is a state in which the mind's faculties are at their best to intuit, to observe, to evaluate, and to discern—a state at which you are your best possible self. It is truly illuminating.

PARTING

It is my hope that I have been that "companion on the way," for each of the people whom I have had the opportunity to listen to, in order to help each one find that miracle. Each opportunity to do so in my life has been a blessing to me. It's all about the Love Motif. And, of course, it works both ways.

There is something within us that knows who we are
and what we are intended to be.

—John Sanford

For more information about Gayle Alexander Vincent
and Anne Vincent's practice or to learn more about
Cottage In the Woods, please contact Anne Alexander
at anne@cottageinthewoods.com

May the road rise to meet you

May the wind be always at your back

May the sun shine warm upon your face

The rains fall soft upon your fields

And until we meet again

May God hold you in the palm of his hand.

—Old Irish Blessing

Written Works Recommended by the Author:

Kahlil Gibran: **The Prophet**

A classic collection of timeless essays written with stunning poetic beauty.

Viktor Frankl: **Man's Search for Meaning**

Frankl's classic chronicling his experience in Nazi concentration camps and his ideas about coping with suffering, finding meaning in that suffering, and the triumph of the human spirit.

Dag Hammarskjold: **Markings**

Sage and spiritual insights from a great public servant and former Secretary General of the United Nations.

Norman Cousins: The Biology of Hope

The former editor of the *Saturday Review* presents his ideas on the effect of hope on physical health.

Frederick Buechner: Listening to Your Life

Writings from a gifted spiritual seeker underlining God's accessibility to man.

Golda Meir: My Life

A rich biography by a great leader bringing the history of Israel to life.

Mildred Cowman: Streams in the Desert

Spiritual inspiration based on ideas that sustained her while working as a missionary in China and Japan.

Anne Morrow Lindbergh: Gift from the Sea

With elegant insights and brilliant metaphor, she explores the relationship between the sea and mental well-being.